PENNED
ZOO POEMS

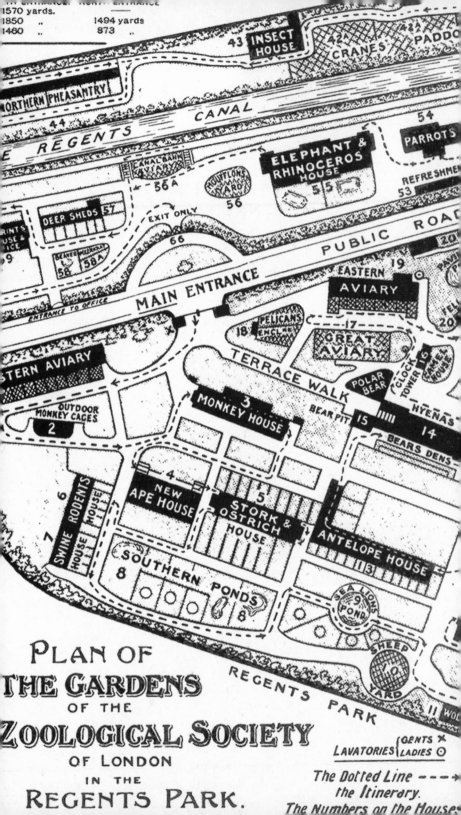

PLAN OF THE GARDENS OF THE ZOOLOGICAL SOCIETY OF LONDON IN THE REGENTS PARK.

Penned

ZOO POEMS

EDITED BY

Stephanie Bolster, Katia Grubisic
and Simon Reader

SIGNAL EDITIONS IS AN IMPRINT OF VÉHICULE PRESS

Published with the generous assistance of the Canada Council for
the Arts, the Book Publishing Industry Development Program of the
Department of Canadian Heritage and the Société de développement des
entreprises culturelles du Québec (SODEC).

Signal series editor: Carmine Starnino

Cover design: J.W. Stewart
Cover photograph, "Hippo, Rotterdam," by Dominic Davies
Frontispiece: Detail from the Guide of the London Zoo, 1904
Set in Minion by Simon Garamond
Printed by Marquis Book Printing Inc.

LIBRARY AND ARCHIVES CANADA CATALOGUING IN PUBLICATION

Penned : zoo poems / edited by Stephanie Bolster,
Katia Grubisic, Simon Reader.

Includes index.

ISBN 978-1-55065-263-5

1. English poetry. 2. Zoo animals—Poetry. I. Bolster, Stephanie
II. Grubisic, Katia III. Reader, Simon
PN6110.A7P45 2009   821.008'0362   C2009-903490-5

Published by Véhicule Press, Montréal, Québec, Canada
www.vehiculepress.com

Distribution in Canada by LitDistCo
www.litdistco.ca

Distribution in U.S. by Independent Publishers Group
www.ipgbook.com

Printed in Canada on 100% post-consumer recycled paper.

Contents

Introduction 9

The Ingenuity of Chain-Link

Introduction

"They look back at the leopard like the leopard."
~Randall Jarrell, "The Woman at the Washington Zoo"

Between the human animal and other animals, between our hairless palm and the fuzzy paw, or the fin, or the leathery-skinned simian hand with its nearly opposable thumbs, there is a pen.... *Penned: Zoo Poems* gathers English-language poems from around the world, spanning over a century of captivity with the worlds inside the cage and out. Our guides on this journey, at times nostalgic, haunting, whimsical and provocative, include emerging and eminent poets—Margaret Atwood, Elizabeth Bishop, Lorna Crozier, Emily Dickinson, Lawrence Ferlinghetti, Gerard Manley Hopkins, A.A. Milne, Al Purdy, A.K. Ramanujan, Matthew Sweeney. The poems themselves are as rich and varied as the species they corral, exploring enclosure, exhibition and the exotic. We wander through the poems of this eclectic anthology as through a zoo, looking back at the animal, to paraphrase Randall Jarrell, like the animal.

This anthology began with an idea—the human examines, and makes art of, already-examined and already-shaped nature—and with the grand ambitions and the naiveté of first-time anthologists: this would be a collection about not only zoos but gardens, with prose as well as poetry, with writing from the earliest known instances of collecting and exhibiting animals and plants, from countries that no longer existed, written in languages that we couldn't read.

Gardens were the first to go. That anthology would be a different one, its concerns less charged; though there is much to be written about botanical imperialism, for example, it takes considerable imagination to lament a geranium's pot-bound existence.

Then, off with prose. Poetry interrogates looking, it tugs at the bars, pries open the cage in infinite ways. In prose fiction, by contrast, zoos tend to be mentioned superficially: as backdrops, in passing similes, with quasi-parental exasperation or with social, and frequently colonial, connotations.

The poems here include work published up to this year, but we had to start somewhere, and so began our search with 1828, when London's Regent's Park opened the first public zoological garden in the English-speaking world. There were fewer nineteenth-century poems than we had hoped to find, and of these, we deemed only a handful suitable. Unsurprisingly, given the novelty of zoos at that time, these poems were either straightforward appreciations or condemnations, or reflective of responses that strike us now as expected or sentimental. Often, the poems were too bound by the styles of their time to hold their weight as poetry.

The final restriction was linguistic, as we realized that including translations not only raised the difficult question of multiple translations—of Rilke's "The Panther," for example—but meant that, unless our research were much more extensive, we would miss all but the most obvious examples of zoo poetry in translation.

Despite three years of scrounging, heaps of recommendations and a call for submissions, not every zoo poem written in English found its way in. No doubt we'll continue to find work we'll wish we'd discovered in time to include. Some poems had to go free, some were too elusive to catch. Perhaps nine out of ten died on the journey or were abandoned, not unlike the ratios of those who hunt, retrieve and cage the real thing.

We decided early on that literary quality would be the most significant criterion for inclusion. This is first a book of good poetry, about zoos. We were not, after all, writing a scholarly book (Randy Malamud's excellent *Reading Zoos* already serves this function) and we wanted none of the blandly thematic inclusions the American poet David Lehman mentions, in his foreword to *The Best American Poetry 2004*—"enough for a poem to be written about zucchini to warrant its inclusion in a volume of vegetable poems." *Penned* is a collection meant to be read, pondered, shared.

Though we generally agreed which poems were most successful— as poems, and as examinations of zoos—most of these were melancholy, if not downright depressing. Any levity tended to be ironic, and while poems intended for children offered some genuine delight, their form and one-note nature often made them uninteresting to an adult readership. Ultimately, we did include some lighter poems for balance, and excluded some excellent poems that tipped the scales too deeply into bleakness. In considering what makes a zoo poem, we've done our best to choose representative specimens written in various emotional registers and forms, during various eras, by writers of various ages and ethnicities and from various countries. (We have retained

the original geographical spelling variants of the poems included.)
The book that you hold in your hands is one of many zoo anthologies
that might have been. These poems don't blindly accept or reject the
zoo; rather, they consider what else the zoo might contain or suggest.

Before the work of the poet or the anthologist begins, the zoo is
already a literary place, and an anthology of sorts. A system designed
to make nature readable, the zoo offers representative examples of
species and even entire ecosystems. Like poetry, the zoo directly con-
fronts us with notions of presentation and representation, with imitation
(think of a mural at the back of the fish tank) and rhetorical tricks
(three tamarins made to stand for the whole rainforest). It should come
as no surprise that many poets have found in the zoo a serious aesthetic
and intellectual habitat.

Many of these are zoo poems only metaphorically, in that they are
about everything but—childhood, dreams, love. Whose is the habitat
of the zoo poem? Even when we found poems explicitly about captive
animals, we often disagreed on the required degree of zooishness.
Would a bird in a cage do? Should we excerpt from bestiaries and longer
poems? And what if the animals were little more than human stand-
ins, their plight reflecting the concerns of human animals—overcrowd-
ing, pollution, constraints, alienation, aggression? As Gwendolyn MacEwen
writes, "in this zoo there are beasts which / like some truths, are far
too true." Isn't that overlay of human truth an additional cage? Can we
write poetry about zoos without becoming the Audubon in Robert
Kroetsch's poem, the artist raising his gun?

Most of us can hear within the zoo gates something like an elegy;
zoos disconnect us from nature even as they claim to offer a substitute
for nature. In the zoo, metaphor itself becomes suspect. "Elephant is
said to be there," Ralph Gustafson writes. Beauty also returns repeatedly
in these poems, often darkly, wearing what Miriam Waddington calls
"a heavy hood and a light head." Other poets, such as Diane Wakoski,
simultaneously admonish and forgive both poets and the zoo:

> some of us have bad vision, are crippled, have defects, and
> our reality is a different one
> ...
> and sometimes it makes us dotty and lonely
> but also it makes us poets.

Some of the poets included here have written numerous zoo poems; we restricted ourselves to a single poem per poet in order to keep the collection as varied as possible. The usual zoological suspects are here: Randall Jarrell's "The Woman at the Washington Zoo," Marianne Moore's "The Monkeys," Sylvia Plath's "Zoo Keeper's Wife." In the case of Ted Hughes, months of debate that leaned in favour of the complex, less commonly anthologized "The Black Rhino" ended, for financial reasons, with the old faithful jaguar. Blake's "The Tyger" stands as an absent presence, a palimpsest over which many of these poems were written.

Befitting the solitary nature of the lyric, there are many poems about close encounters with particular animals, such as William Stafford's "The Coyote in the Zoo," in which the animal looks back. And in keeping with the tragic predilections of many poets, there are several poems here about zoos during or after war. From a handful of escape poems we kept only P.J. Kavanagh's "Goldie *sapiens*," finding others too melodramatic or too little concerned with the zoo. Poems about elephants are also common, the intelligence, sensitivity, and size of these animals serving as emotionally stirring representatives of ill-fated zoo creatures.

Cheery zoo poems are easier to spot; we found few in our research, and fewer still that were good enough to include. Miriam Waddington's "Wonderful Country" distinguishes itself with an edge: of swans, she writes, "Let them be, they will make pillows soft as sleep, / And sleep deep as death."

Finally, although many children's poems adopt the voices of animals, Alvin Greenberg's "we are that stuffed cat that guards the hats" and Gertrude Halstead's "panther" are the only poems we've included that overtly do so. The paucity of speaking animals may reflect poets' discomfort with voice appropriation, the perceived impossibility of imagining oneself as a caged animal, the perceived sentimentality of doing so, or the need for the observer to remain an observer.

Rather than organize the poems by species or publication date, we've ordered them more intuitively: some are placed to highlight their contrast with surrounding poems, while others are grouped for similarity of tone or style. *Penned* demarcates three different, though fairly permeable, realities: the first section, "The Ingenuity of Chain-Link," considers the zoo from within. Poems about specific zoos or species share a documentary quality, and convey to the reader the poet's initial awe or surprise, often in an extravaganza of image and allusion—Julie Sheehan's polar bear is doing a Busby Berkeley routine; Stephen Burt's lemurs are "hot / and concave in their inappropriate coats"; Selima Hill's parrots pile at her feet "like dying socks."

The second section, "The One That Looks Away," shifts the perspective from the beheld to the beholders, with both, in Countee Cullen's words, "caught in a vastness beyond our sight to see." These poems can be funny, as when Carol Ann Duffy's Mrs Darwin throws evolution back at her husband; they frame love stories, or speak for zookeepers; or they are reflective, as for Tobias Hill, who muses,

> Cages leave nothing except time
> to think, and nothing else to think
>
> except that all cages have holes.

In the third section, "Things All Shaped Like Tigers," the zoo zooms in on these holes, delving into the imagination. With Sasha West, we dream "of sleeping in the elephant's ear"; in Peter Meinke's "Running with the Hyenas" and Michael Van Walleghen's "The Elephant in Winter," among others, the zoo is the site of an epiphany. We end with Lisa Jarnot's romping "They Loved These Things Too." Its final phrase rings true, for although there is much to question, to mourn, to fear, and to deplore in zoos, we love things shaped like tigers, and we love the zoo.

Stephanie Bolster, Katia Grubisic, Simon Reader
Montreal, May 2009

The Ingenuity of Chain-Link

Joanie Mackowski

THE ZOO

Fully clothed and delighted between bars
we watch it bare

its teeth, pacing in cages, naked in furs
(ah, a peacock's tail unfurls

a wall of eyes!), and we, too, brave the wild—but beware:
this wilderness may overpower us

just with the strength it wields to be so self-contained.
A small crowd taken

in, four giraffes traverse an arid lot.
Their bodies undulate

as if underwater, their heads float on the sky like lotuses—
while nearby, motionless,

zebras breathe in the breeze, their stripes
ever so slightly rippling.

It's high noon, and overcast, besides,
but scarlet ibises

set a flock of bright orange suns; they perch
in a freestanding screened porch,

and five toddlers, linked together with a rope,
are told not to poke

their vegetable fingers through the chain-link
fence, for behind it lounges

a tiger, whose eyebrows reverberate
as her blasé tongue browses

the velvet envelopes between her new-moon
claws. A dingy emu

now cradles in her womb three bright green eggs,
(or so the placard says),

while antelopes leap over opales-
cent sun rays; impalas

wade in pools, and diamond patterns, bird-scratches,
mark the backs of my chapped

hands.... At the zoo, essence and ornament
meet. Is it mental

effort that keeps the well-intentioned soul
uncorrupted by this raw

nature, this ostentatious camouflage?
Or does the leisurely

daydream, half forgot, that weaves gracefully
through the overblown grass

at the base of our brains really protect
us more? There, brown ducks

escape a widening ring, and the slate-gray
water of a grassy

pool suddenly congeals into a terrible,
dripping Gibraltar:

the hippo shows his eyes and leather armor
and sinks again. Amour?—

lunatic spasms of a kookaburra
buckle in the air;

the bird itself I cannot see; its idi-
osyncratic, giddy

call hovers generally beneath the outspread
wings of the chestnut

eagle, regal (though tied by the ankle
to a wooden anchor),

who splays his jagged feathers like the petals
of a rose. Bedazzled,

I amble through the zoo lazily
as the dazed animals.

An appendix on my memory swells, and my
pace slows, muscles

contract—prepare to spring (what ambergris
now grows in me?): some animals are angry,

I think, to be kept in cages,
but which is stronger,

the ingenuity of chain-link
(look!) or fascination?

Stephen Burt

AT THE PROVIDENCE ZOO

Like the Beatles arriving from Britain,
the egret's descent on the pond
takes the reeds and visitors by storm:
it is a reconstructed marsh
environment, the next
best thing to living out your wild life.

*

Footbridges love the past.
And like the Roman questioner who learned
"the whole of the Torah while standing on one leg,"
flamingos are pleased to ignore us. It is not known
whether that Roman could learn to eat upside-down,
by dragging his tremendous head through streams.

*

Comical, stately, the newly-watched tortoises
mate; one pushes the other over the grass,
their hemispheres clicking, on seven legs
in toto. Together they make
a Sydney Opera House,
a concatenation of anapests, almost a waltz.

*

Confined if not preserved,
schoolteachers, their charges, vigilant lemurs, wrens
and prestidigitating tamarins,
and dangerous badgers like dignitaries stare
at one another, hot
and concave in their inappropriate coats.

*

Having watched a boa
eat a rat alive,
the shortest child does as she was told—
looks up, holds the right hand
of the buddy system, and stands,
as she explains it, "still as a piece of pie."

Irving Layton

AT THE BARCELONA ZOO

When reading Heraclitos at the zoo
elephants, bisons, dromedaries
are a solid deception,
a fleshy denial of the flux
he's forever going on about

So are trained dolphins that blow trumpets;
do you mean to say the water buffalo
couldn't flop into the same stream twice
if he had a mind to? I'll bet he can. Anyhow
of one thing I'm sure: he loses no sleep over it

It's the delicate pink flamingoes
with their brittle long pencil-like legs
that get me: feathered shapes of flame
that even as they move flicker out into darkness
or Anaximander's *apeiron*

It's mice, skunks, rabbits, ocelots
and the infinite variety of tenuous blooms
that speak to me of joyous impermanency
and of the Artist-God who shapes and plays with them
as I have shaped these words into a poem

A.K. Ramanujan

ZOO GARDENS REVISITED

Once flamingoes reminded me of long-legged aunts in white cottons, and black-faced monkeys of grave lowbrow uncles with movable scalps and wrinkled long black hands. Now animals remind me only of animals,

orangutans of only orangutans, and of tuberculosis in the Delhi Zoo. And the symmetric giraffe in London that split in two trying to mount a coy female who gave him no quarter.

Visitors no longer gape at ostriches, so they tell me, but shrewdly set their tail feathers on fire with lighter fluid and cigarette lighters. So ostriches in zoos no longer hide their heads in sand as they do in proverbs.

Some, they say, feed bananas to the dying race of ring-tailed monkeys, bananas with small exquisite needles in them. So monkeys in zoos no longer eat bananas as they still do in temple cities and Jungle Books.

Tigresses, I hear, go barren, or superintended by curious officials adulterate their line with half-hearted lions to breed experimental ligers and tions as they breed pomatoes and totatoes in botanical gardens.

Eight-foot tigers yawn away their potency. Till yesterday, they burned bright in the forests of the night. It was a way of living. Now their eyes are embers in the ash. A slight movement of the eyelash flicks the ash.

The other day in Mysore a chimp named Subbu was paralysed neck down. He couldn't lift his chipped blue enamel mug to his lips and slurp his tea any more nor pout his lips to puff at his cigar.

The Society of Animal Lovers babysat for Subbu in shifts till in the small hours of the third morning he bit the sweetest lady of them all in a fury his protectors could not understand.

Lord of lion face, boar snout, and fish eyes, killer of killer cranes, shepherd of rampant elephants, devour my lambs, devour them whole, save them in the zoo garden ark of your belly.

Marianne Moore

THE MONKEYS

winked too much and were afraid of snakes. The zebras, supreme in
their abnormality; the elephants with their fog-colored skin
   and strictly practical appendages
      were there, the small cats; and the parakeet—
         trivial and humdrum on examination, destroying
      bark and portions of the food it could not eat.

I recall their magnificence, now not more magnificent
than it is dim. It is difficult to recall the ornament,
   speech, and precise manner of what one might
      call the minor acquaintances twenty
         years back; but I shall not forget him—that Gilgamesh among
      the hairy carnivora—that cat with the

wedge-shaped, slate-gray marks on its forelegs and the resolute tail,
astringently remarking, "They have imposed on us with their pale
   half-fledged protestations, trembling about
      in inarticulate frenzy, saying
         it is not for us to understand art; finding it
      all so difficult, examining the thing

as if it were inconceivably arcanic, as symmet-
rically frigid as if it had been carved out of chrysoprase
   or marble—strict with tension, malignant
      in its power over us and deeper
         than the sea when it proffers flattery in exchange for hemp,
      rye, flax, horses, platinum, timber, and fur."

John Wain

AU JARDIN DES PLANTES

The gorilla lay on his back,
One hand cupped under his head,
Like a man.

Like a labouring man tired with work,
A strong man with his strength burnt away
In the toil of earning a living.

Only of course he was not tired out with work,
Merely with boredom; his terrible strength
All burnt away by prodigal idleness.

A thousand days, and then a thousand days,
Idleness licked away his beautiful strength,
He having no need to earn a living.

It was all laid on, free of charge.
We maintained him, not for doing anything,
But for being what he was.

And so that Sunday morning he lay on his back,
Like a man, like a worn-out man,
One hand cupped under his terrible hard head.

Like a man, like a man,
One of those we maintain, not for doing anything,
But for being what they are.

A thousand days, and then a thousand days,
With everything laid on, free of charge,
They cup their heads in prodigal idleness.

E.E. Cummings

30

the silently little blue elephant shyly(he was terri
bly
warped by his voyage from every to no)who
still stands still as found some lost thing(like a
curtain on which tiny the was painted in round
blue but quite now it's swirly and foldish so only through)the
little blue elephant at the zoo(jumbled
to queer this what that a here and
there a peers at you)has(elephant the blue)put some just
a now and now little the(on his quiet
head his magical shoulders him doll
self)hay completely thus or that wispily
is to say according to his perfect
satisfaction vanishing from a this world into bigger
much some out of(not visible to us)whom only his dream
ing own soul looks
and
the is all floatful and remembering

Alison Calder

DON'T THINK OF AN ELEPHANT

Drop your finger, blind, onto the map, and you will not hit
an elephant.
Yet they say the first bomb dropped on Berlin in World War II
killed the only elephant in the Berlin Zoo,
the logic of his death no stranger
than his transplanted life beside the statues
of the Tiergarten's Elephant Gate. By cart, by ship, by train,
commercial lines reel him into paddocks he could never have imagined,
penned up in the wrong place, wrong time.
At the Gate his doubled likeness, hobbled, carries emperors
over cobblestones, escapes the zoo's walls
to annex the city. Behold
an image trampling on its model, heading
straight for blank space at the centre
of the flag. Here the lion, here the rhino,
the animals of empire,
charging.

Meanwhile, our elephant is only flesh.
As his granite twins, bejewelled, command the street,
he flaps his ears, eats candy. In the shade
he naps, swats flies, ambles pleasantly along
the inside of his fence, takes peanuts.
Drinking from his curled trunk,
he lifts his head. A thick-skinned beast
drops toward him from the sky.

David McFadden

ELEPHANTS

Knoxville, San Diego, Winnipeg, Buffalo, Granby, Toronto: a list
of zoos I've visited this year. And anyone could see the gorillas at the
Toronto Zoo were conscious, deliberate philosophers with no vocabulary,
sitting in the glass house pondering ambiguity, paradox and the absolutes.
At Granby the gorillas were of a decidedly lower class. I hope they don't
read this. Two big ones studiously ignored a tossed banana for several
tense minutes until finally the male broke down and flickered with
interest and the female leaped from her perch, pounced on the banana,
then ate it herself while the male tried to pretend he didn't care. And
an American eagle attacked his mate over a gerbil tossed in their cage.

Viciously too, all heaven in a rage. But when I held out a handful of
nuts to the bull elephant he took only half, then slowly backed up so his
mate could have the remainder. The eyes of these sad spiritual lovers in
leg chains checked to see if I understood and appreciated their little gesture
of kindness and love, and I felt I'd been blessed by the Pope. They knew
there was nothing I could do to free them, though when two doves were
presented to Pope John Paul II in Montreal he released them and they
didn't fly away, just sat there in transcendental splendour in the middle
of crowded Olympic Stadium, little haloes radiant. And people who live
in the vicinity of the Granby Zoo when you get to know them will shyly
confide in you that late at night after they turn off the television they lie
in bed listening to and feeling the earth and sky quivering and murmuring
with the mammoth heartbreaking hour-long orgasms of the elephants.

Judith Beveridge

THE DOMESTICITY OF GIRAFFES

She languorously swings her tongue
like a black leather strap as she chews
and endlessly licks the wire for salt
blown in from the harbour.
Bruised-apple eyed she ruminates
towards the tall buildings
she mistakes for a herd:
her gaze has the loneliness of smoke.

I think of her graceful on her plain—
one long-legged mile after another.
I see her head framed in a leafy bonnet
or balloon-bobbing in trees.
Her hide's a paved garden of orange
against wild bush. In the distance, running
she could be a big slim bird just before flight.

Here, a wire-cripple—
legs stark as telephone poles
miles from anywhere.
She circles the pen, licks the wire,
mimics a gum-chewing audience
in the stained underwear of her hide.
This shy Miss Marigold rolls out her tongue

like the neck of a dying bird.
I offer her the fresh salt of my hand
and her tongue rolls over it
in sensual agony, as it must
over the wire, hour after bitter hour.
Now, the bull indolently
lets down his penis like a pink gladiolus
drenching the concrete.

She thrusts her tongue under his rich stream
to get moisture for her thousandth chew.

Ted Hughes

THE JAGUAR

The apes yawn and adore their fleas in the sun.
The parrots shriek as if they were on fire, or strut
Like cheap tarts to attract the stroller with the nut.
Fatigued with indolence, tiger and lion

Lie still as the sun. The boa-constrictor's coil
Is a fossil. Cage after cage seems empty, or
Stinks of sleepers from the breathing straw.
It might be painted on a nursery wall.

But who runs like the rest past these arrives
At a cage where the crowd stands, stares, mesmerized,
As a child at a dream, at a jaguar hurrying enraged
Through prison darkness after the drills of his eyes

On a short fierce fuse. Not in boredom—
The eye satisfied to be blind in fire,
By the bang of blood in the brain deaf the ear—
He spins from the bars, but there's no cage to him

More than to the visionary his cell:
His stride is wildernesses of freedom:
The world rolls under the long thrust of his heel.
Over the cage floor the horizons come.

P.J. Kavanagh

GOLDIE *SAPIENS*

When Goldie the golden eagle escaped from the Zoo
All the world went to Regents Park and we went too.
There he was, with an air of depression, a sooty hunch,
Digesting the grey-eyed merganser he had for lunch.
Under him children and coppers and mothers and fathers
And bare-kneed ornithologists with cameras
Hanging down to their ankles and lovers and others
Peeling damp cellophane from sandwiches stand and wait.
While running around in sad moustaches Keepers,
Hopelessly, like H.M. Bateman characters,
Shoo Pekes away from buckets of eagle bait.
Really, this bird was a National Occasion!
The Evening Standard published an hourly bulletin
As though it was getting in training for Sir Winston.
And none of us knew what we most wanted to see,
The Keepers allowed to go home or the bird to go free.
There was an appalling sense of a happy ending too—
Goldie was free but he kept an eye cocked on his Zoo.
Just then there started up where Goldie was,
A thrush fit to burst but we didn't listen because
We were enjoying the sight we'd come to see—
The only free eagle in captivity.
Later that evening the Nation breathed a sigh.
Goldie like us, Goldie the human and sage,
With tail between talons, had lallopped back to the cage.

Selima Hill

PARROTS

I am surrounded by parrots.
They leave their chopped tomatoes on my head.
They pile at my feet like dying socks.

Their lettuce-coloured shoulders are so heavenly
the people at the zoo go mad about them.
One of them is looking in my eyes,

and saying, *What's the matter, Billy?* (meaning me).
Catch them, someone, take them back to Paradise,
they're giving me a terrible disease.

Gerard Manley Hopkins

THE CAGED SKYLARK

As a dare-gale skylark scanted in a dull cage
    Man's mounting spirit in his bone-house, mean house, dwells—
    That bird beyond the remembering his free fells;
This in drudgery, day-labouring-out life's age.

Though aloft on turf or perch or poor low stage,
    Both sing sometímes the sweetest, sweetest spells,
    Yet both droop deadly sómetimes in their cells
Or wring their barriers in bursts of fear or rage.

Not that the sweet-fowl, song-fowl, needs no rest—
Why, hear him, hear him babble and drop down to his nest,
    But his own nest, wild nest, no prison.

Man's spirit will be flesh-bound when found at best,
But uncumberèd: meadow-down is not distressed
    For a rainbow footing it nor he for his bónes rísen.

Larry Levis

WAKING WITH SOME ANIMALS

Waking, I remember that
the lion is pacing the shadowy zoo.
The elephants sleep standing on all fours,
wearing huge roses fastened deep within their ears.
And things are kicked over in the darkness.

Jan Conn

THE TIGERS OF PARAMARIBO

are more radiant than Borges' blue dream tigers,
and there are five of them,
indolent, breath-taking,
their carnivorous nature evident
in every stipple of muscle, each stripe and counter-stripe,
as though they themselves were shadow / sun / shadow.

Early morning, hot and muggy, a suburb
on the outskirts of Paramaribo, uncut grass,
nothing alive in the Reptile House,
and one horse slouching its swayback way easily
down the path past the cage, the black bars casting
more shadows, striping the tiger stripes,

and a tall serious woman, meditating on
tigerness,
unable to get past the first swallow of raw antelope,
sketches, takes detailed notes…

Then the tigers, all five at once, crouch
belly-flat, ears down,
and rush *en masse* as though on cue
at the horse.
They leap up, seemingly bending the bars,
fall back, leap again

and the man with the camera runs toward the woman,
thinking the tigers have been provoked
by her black-and-white zebra leggings

but she has now managed
to swallow the whole antelope
and slipped between the bars, calmly
looking out at him, licking her massive
paws.

Gertrude Halstead

panther

leopard in the black color phase
       the day   hot
       i slept
       the night   moonless
       i left the den
       to hunt
       that black night
       and i   as black
       as night   why
       that night
       that black night
       and i   as black
       as that night
       and i   as black
       as that moonless night
              caught
       that night   why
       that night of my hunt
              the hunter
       hunted   caught
       behind bars
       that black night
       and eyes   all day
that   day   night
and   eyes   all
day   eyes   between
bars   and   eyes
behind   bars   cold

bars	bare	bars
bare	as	tree
trunks	yet	not
tree	trunks	no
more	trees	no
more	forest	only
bars	back	and
forth	forest	of
bars	back	and
forth	right	and
left	nothing	left
nothing	right	round
and	round	walls
in	back	bars
in	front	forest
of	bars	no
more	forest	no
more	trees	only
walls	bars	eyes
i	i	i

Molly Peacock

THE SNAKE

As if all her vertebrae wore tiny
well-designed internal shoes which deftly
writhe as the shoes of commuters writhe
all lined up on a down escalator,
so the thigh-size python stores herself up,
then crawls from the limb's cuff
through her glassed-in world,

                       painted
with a brilliant mural, giving the sense
of false home that murals in offices do—abated,
foreshortened, her screened background the tense
quiver of colors on terminal screens.
Her cage is her office; the zoo is her work.
She performs masterfully her routine
as tenured civil serpent, trained,
restrained.

          But what is her redemption,
if redemption is a being's recognition
of its limits? Hers are mere inches
of the pole she turns around on, her life
an exhibition on bald, denuded branches.
I hope her brain is very large,
her only hope to put a mind in charge,
capacious in imagining her prayer
of what should be there.

Marianne Boruch

LUNCH

The zoo. So one thinks up from
the amoeba, way ahead to one's great-grandchildren
someday or no day. Then back where old
photographs live, those minutes
locked in the ice
of someone's remembering, some uncle
with a camera. But the zoo—here!—
is very matter-of-fact: warm bodies (monkeys,
zebras, any moving thing
with beak, with feathers) versus
the flashing cold and/or hot ones: the bite-the-dirt-
for-all-we-do-wrong ones
or the soft-bellied frog or the salamander flattened,
shrunk, puffed out, its legs, arms,
sweet little claws completely
not a snake, having lured no one and nothing.

I was saying: consider the metal bars. To keep
such wonders in, to keep us—small wonders—out.
Almost noon, some uniformed someone
turns up with bananas, seeds,
fetal pigs, apples, the works. How not
to love this guy?—his trusty
indifference, his all-right-another-day-of-it
shrug and off-key whistle. The animals
look up. *Something is about to happen.* Food

does that. In this saddest of worlds, think
lunch! and an ocean of hope
rides over us. Is it hope? And too cheap? This
metaphor filling the moment? the mind?
the life finally and exactly? I mean
the guy's coming closer, the one
with a bucket. And a shovel.

Jeni Couzyn

A ZOO SEQUENCE

Yellow Baboon

The yellow baboon
his organ a pink dying stalk
masturbates, legs spread wide
without interest—as one would casually
peel a banana
looking around him.
When his moment of
passion comes, I detect a faint
irritation
as he hooks the toes of his two feet together
and straightens his knees.
Then he lifts the white fruit from the limp
stalk, and eats it
rudely, without enjoyment, dipping his finger
carefully to scoop the last drops.

Squirrel

See the way a caged squirrel
at feeding time
will tear the nut open
his small face trembling over the
stainless steel dish.

Sea-Eagle

—Why are his wings so big?
   Why?
Because they are.
—But why?
Because he is heavy
he has to go
up in the air.
—Why does he sit
   with his wings
     stretched out like that
     filling his cage?

   Wolf

   Savage things asleep
   look gentle
   and is this softly breathing the
   enemy, who stole your sheep?

Rhinoceros

Inside that lump of granite
blood flows
cells break
somewhere you are.
Behind that small black hole
images float again
somewhere in there I am
somewhere, where you are.

The Small Insect House

All these small creatures
attend to themselves
the millipede very slowly
sucks tiny parasite flecks from
his long black shell
combing it carefully with his
million fine legs—
Stick insect
hermit crab
praying mantis that was
sacred to bushmen.

Lemur

Lemur fingers glass with
small paws
where frosted light
falls gently.

A.A. Milne

AT THE ZOO

There are lions and roaring tigers, and enormous
      camels and things,
There are biffalo-buffalo-bisons, and a great big
      bear with wings,
There's a sort of a tiny potamus, and a tiny
      nosserus too—
But *I* gave buns to the elephant when *I* went down
      to the Zoo!

There are badgers and bidgers and bodgers, and a
      Superintendent's House,
There are masses of goats, and a Polar, and different
      kinds of mouse,
And I think there's a sort of a something which is
      called a wallaboo—
But *I* gave buns to the elephant when *I* went down
      to the Zoo!

If you try to talk to the bison, he never quite
      understands;
You can't shake hands with a mingo—he doesn't
      like shaking hands.
And lions and roaring tigers *hate* saying, "How do
      you do?"—
But *I* give buns to the elephant when *I* go down to
      the Zoo!

Henry Lee (attrib.)

THINGS NEW AT THE ZOO!

Go, people, and pay all
To see the she-gayal
   That Bartlett has had brought from the Indies;
And the wolves from Thibet,
Which mammals we bet
   Will raise in their dens fearful shindies.

The arctonyx snout
Is the newest thing out,
   The first ever heard of in London;
A Panolian deer,
Fresh to this hemisphere,
   Awaits you, your beer and your bun done.

There's a pigeon that sings,
And one with bronze wings,
   Polyplectrous and likewise a Loris;
A monkey—men tell us
To call it Entellus—
   The charge but a bob at the door is.

There are demoiselle cranes
To be seen for your pains,
   With six or eight of the tortoise;
And a Hemipode ends
This list of new friends
   The *Marian Moore* lately brought us:

No, stay, there are pelicans—
Rhyme to them Helicon's
   Verse-helping fount might supply us;
But a New River draught,

Teetotally quaffed,
   Is all the liqueur we have by us.

So the Floreat "Zoo,"
Both old beasts and new;
   And when you have seen all its treasures,
Take an ice or a tartlet,
And thank Mr. Bartlett
   For adding so much to your pleasures.

Frederick Locker-Lampson

THE BEAR PIT

In the Zoological Gardens

*It seems that poor Bruin has never had peace
'Twixt bald men in Bethel, and wise men in grease.*
                    –Old Adage

We liked the Bear's serio-comical face,
As he loll'd with a lazy, a lumbering grace;
Said Slyboots to me (just as if *she* had none),
"Papa, let's give Bruin a bit of your bun."

Says I, "A plum bun might please wistful old Bruin,
He can't eat the stone that the cruel boy threw in;
Stick *yours* on the point of mamma's parasol,
And then he will climb to the top of the pole.

"Some Bears have got two legs, and some have got more,
Be good to old Bears if they've no legs or four;
Of duty to age you should never be careless, —
My dear, I am bald, and I soon may be hairless!

"The gravest aversion exists among bears
From rude forward persons who give themselves airs,
We know how some graceless young people were maul'd
For plaguing a Prophet, and calling him *bald*.

"Strange ursine devotion! Their dancing-days ended,
Bears die to 'remove' what, in life, they defended:
They succour'd the Prophet, and, since that affair,
The bald have a painful regard for the bear."

My Moral! Small people may read it, and run.
(The Child has my moral—the bear has my bun.)—

Forbear to give pain, if it's only in jest,
And care to think pleasure a phantom at best.
A paradox too—none can hope to attach it,
Yet if you pursue it you'll certainly catch it.

Julie Sheehan

POLAR BEAR IN THE CENTRAL PARK ZOO

Watched, captivating, he swims to the rocky shelf
and berths a beat before pushing off with plate-sized
foot, belly up, yellow head plowing a watery furrow.

He soaks. A forepaw backstrokes the water once,
idly, but with force enough to speed his streamlined
bulk across the dole of open sea he's fathomed utterly.

He dives as if tethered, submerged body spread and flat
against the viewing glass, mounted momentarily, a trophy
hide on the lodge wall. Watchers shriek, but he moves on

his fixed orbit, water-logged planet, up to the rock, a push,
one backstroke, dive, eyes closed the while. His swim,
compulsory as a Busby Berkeley routine, has captivated

the bear too, or made him half-captive, while the other half,
repeating his invention move for move, seeks a different
outcome: a new mercy, colder, austere; more genuine ice.

Walter Pavlich

SARAJEVO BEAR

The last animal

        In the Sarajevo Zoo

A bear

        Died of starvation

Because the leaves

        Had fallen

From the trees

        Because

The air was

        Getting colder

So the snipers

        Could more easily see

The few remaining people

        Who were trying to

Feed it.

William Stafford

THE COYOTE IN THE ZOO

A yellow eye meets mine;
I suddenly know, too late,
the land outside belongs
to the one that looks away.

The One That Looks Away

Tobias Hill

THE SOUND OF CAGES

We walk each other home
eating takeaway food.

Licking the guttered mustard
from the warm bones
of wrists and hands. The lit

plinths of Docklands
are behind us, and across the park
comes the sound of zoo cages,

the crash of big animals
moving against small walls.
Cages leave nothing except time
to think, and nothing else to think

except that all cages have holes.
At nights, two escaped eagle owls
hunt our tenemented blocks

from the grey cupolas of St Paul's
to the falafel stalls of Camden.

Tall as children,
their cries bring me awake

without understanding. I listen
with my eyes open.

There is the sound of fire engines
across postcodes, and sometimes
soft voices at corners,
quiet as an ambush, and sometimes

a whistling in the dark,
cold and at ease in the stone
streets. Whistling home
with meat, and without quarantine.

Emily Dickinson

1206

The Show is not the Show
But they that go—
Menagerie to me
My Neighbor be—
Fair Play—
Both went to see—

Carol Frost

THE ST. LOUIS ZOO

The isle is full of noises,
Sounds, and sweet air... sometimes voices.
                    –The Tempest

High, yellow, coiled, and weighting the branch like an odd piece of
            fruit, a snake slept
by the gate, in the serpent house. I walked around the paths hearing

hushed air, piecemeal remarks, and the hoarse voice of the keeper
            spreading cabbage
and pellets in the elephant compound—"Hungry, are you? There's a
            girl.

How's Pearl?" A clucking music, then silence again crept past me
on the waters of the duck pond. Birds with saffron wings in the flight cage

and flamingos the color of mangoes, even their webbed feet red-
            orange, made so
"by the algae they ingest," as angels are made of air—some bickered,

some were tongue-tied, some danced on one leg in the honeyed light.
I thought of autumn as leaves scattered down. Nearby, closed away

in his crude beginnings in a simulated rain forest, the gorilla pulled
            out handfuls
of grass, no Miranda to teach him to speak, though he was full of
            noises
and rank air after swallowing. Smooth rind and bearded husks lay
            about him.
His eyes were ingots when he looked at me.

In late-summer air thick with rose and lily, I felt the old malevolence;
the snake tonguing the air, as if to tell me of its dreaming:—birds of
        paradise

gemming a pond; the unspooling; soft comings on, soft, soft
gestures, twisted and surreptitious; the shock; the taste; the kingdom.

In something more than words, *You are the snake, snake coils in you,*
it said. Do you think anyone knows its own hunger as well as the
        snake?

Why am I not just someone alive? When did Spirit tear me
to see how void of blessing I was? The snake hesitated, tasting dusk's
        black honey,

to feel if it was still good. And through its swoon
it knew it. Leaf, lichen, the least refinements, and the perfection.

Jean Garrigue

FALSE COUNTRY OF THE ZOO

We are large with pity, slow and awkward
In the false country of the zoo.
For the beasts our hearts turn over and sigh,
With the gazelle we long to look eye to eye,
Laughter at the stumbling, southern giraffes
Urges our anger, righteous despair.
As the hartebeest plunges, giddy, eccentric,
From out of the courtyard into his stall,
We long to seize his forehead's steep horns
Which are like the staves of a lyre.
Fleeter than greyhounds the hartebeest
Long-muzzled, small-footed, and shy.
Another runner, the emu, is even better
At kicking. Oh, the coarse chicken feet
Of this bird reputed a fossil!
His body, deep as a table,
Droops gracelessly downwise,
His small head shakes like an old woman's eye.
The emu, the ostrich, the cassowary
Continue to go on living their lives
In conditions unnatural to them
And in relations most strange
Remain the same.
As for the secretary bird,
Snake-killer, he suggests
A mischievous bird-maker.
Like a long-legged boy in short pants
He runs teetering, legs far apart,
On his toes, part gasping girl.
What thought him up, this creature
Eminently equipped by his nervous habits
To kill venomous snakes with his strong
Horny feet, first jumping on them

And then leaping away?
At the reptile and monkey houses
Crowds gather to enjoy the ugly
But mock the kangaroo who walks like a cripple.

In the false country of the zoo,
Where Africa is well represented
By Australia,
The emu, the ostrich and cassowary
Survive like kings, poor antiquated strays,
Deceased in all but vestiges,
Who did not have to change, preserved
In their peculiarities by rifts,
From emigration barred.
Now melancholy, like old continents
Unmodified and discontinued, they
Remain by some discreet permission
Like older souls too painfully handicapped.
Running birds who cannot fly,
Whose virtue is their liability,
Whose stubborn very resistance is their sorrow.
See, as they run, how we laugh
At the primitive, relic procedure.

In the false country of the zoo
Grief is well represented there
By those continents of the odd
And outmoded, Africa and Australia.
Sensation is foremost at a zoo—
The sensation of gaping at the particular:
The striped and camouflaged,
The bear, wallowing in his anger,
The humid tiger wading in a pool.
As for those imports
From Java and India,
The pale, virginal peafowl,
The stork, cracking his bill against a wall,

The peacock, plumes up, though he walks as if weighted
—All that unconscionable tapestry—
Till a wind blows the source of his pride
And it becomes his embarrassment,
The eye, plunged in sensation, closes.
Thought seizes the image. This shrieking
Jungle of spot, stripe, orange
Blurs. The oil from the deer's eye
That streaks like a tear his cheek
Seems like a tear, is, is,
As our love and our pity are, are.

James Dickey

ENCOUNTER IN THE CAGE COUNTRY

What I was would not work
For them all, for I had not caught
The lion's eye. I was walking down

The cellblock in green glasses   and came
At last to the place where someone was hiding
His spots in his black hide.

Unchangeably they were there,
Driven in as by eyes
Like mine, his darkness ablaze

In the stinking sun of the beast house.
Among the crowd, he found me
Out   and dropped his bloody snack

And came to the perilous edge
Of the cage, where the great bars tremble
Like wire. All Sunday ambling stopped,

The curved cells tightened around
Us all   as we saw he was watching only
Me. I knew the stage was set, and I began

To perform   first saunt'ring   then stalking
Back and forth like a sentry   faked
As if to run   and at one brilliant move

I made as though drawing a gun from my hip-
bone, the bite-sized children broke
Up   changing their concept of laughter,

But none of this changed his eyes, or changed
My green glasses. Alert, attentive,
He waited for what I could give him:

My moves   my throat   my wildest love,
The eyes behind my eyes. Instead, I left
Him, though he followed me right to the end

Of concrete. I wiped my face, and lifted off
My glasses. Light blasted the world of shade
Back under every park bush   the crowd

Quailed from me   I was inside and out
Of myself   and something was given a life-
mission to say to me hungrily over

And over and over   *your moves are exactly right*
For a few things in this world: we know you
When you come, Green Eyes, Green Eyes.

Sujata Bhatt

KANKARIA LAKE

Sometimes the nine-year-old boy
finds it difficult
to believe this is water.

It is more like skin;
a reptile's skin—
wrinkled and rough as a crocodile's
       and green.

Bacterial green, decomposed
green—opaque and dull.

As if the lake
were a giant crocodile
he couldn't see the ends of.

Kankaria Lake is on the way
to the Ahmedabad Zoo.
Sundays he always walks across
the bridge over the lake.

In the distance he can see
a small park bordered
       by the water—dry grass
struggles to grow against the scummy lake.
The park seems always deserted.

Sometimes a gardener
or a homeless man
or a wandering storyteller
would fall asleep on the grass
          too close to the lake—
and soon enough the newspapers

would report about how
the crocodiles had devoured
yet another careless man.

The boy thinks he would like to witness
                            such an event.

But then, would he try
            to save the man?

He's not sure.

Or would he just watch
to see how a crocodile eats?

Would the man's legs go first
            or the arms
            or the stomach?

The boy imagines the lake
overpopulated with crocodiles
who never have enough to eat—
for he doesn't believe any fish
could live in such water.

There are hardly any trees
near the lake; no friendly monkeys
who would throw fruits down
to the crocodiles, as they do
            in one old story....

Kankaria Lake had also become
the most popular place
for suicides—That was a fact
which felt more like science-fiction
                            to him.

On those Sunday afternoon
          family outings
he stops
in the middle of the bridge
and leans out
     towards the lake,
now and then sticking his legs out
through the railing
hoping at least one crocodile
will surface,
     raise its head.

But no.
Nothing ever happens.
Sometimes the wind pokes
the lake, making murky ripples.
But the crocodiles prefer
to remain hidden below.
How do they breathe?
     He worries.

In the end he was
always marched off
disappointed to the zoo
where he faced sullen animals
sometimes crouched far away
in the darkest part of the cage,
frightened in
     their festering skins.

Susan Howe

FLANDERS

On Sunday, December 7, 1941, I went with my father to the zoo in Delaware Park even now so many years after there is always for me the fact of this treasured memory of togetherness before he enlisted in the army and went away to Europe. On that Sunday in Buffalo the usually docile polar bears roved restlessly back and forth around the simulated rocks caves and waterfall designed to keep brute force fenced off even by menace of embrace so many zoo animals are accounted fierce. I recall there were three though I could be wrong because I was a deep and nervous child with the north wind of the fairy story ringing in my ears as well as direct perception. Three bears running around rocks as if to show how modern rationalism springs from barbarism and with such noise to call out boldly boldly ventured is half won. Three bears splashing each other and others gathered at the iron railing as though we hadn't been enjoying liberty its checks and balances. Daddy held on tightly to my hand because animals do communicate in a state resembling dissociation so a prepared people will rid the settlement of ice deities identified with rivers they cause animism. Everyone talking of war in those days. Enough to weigh against love. Animals sense something about ruin I think he said our human spirits being partly immaterial at that prefigured time though we didn't know then how free will carries us past to be distance waiting for another meeting a true relation.

Historical imagination gathers in the missing

Mary Noonan

AT THE ZOO

He took me mainly to places of leave-taking—
Bahnhof Grunewald (Auschwitz, Belsen)
the grave of Heinrich von Kleist at the Wannsee
and airy galleries hung with paintings of death—

pulled me, running, through the tunnels of the S-Bahn
as if our lives depended on some east-bound train
we were about to miss. But the aquarium stopped us
in our tracks, we spent hours there, days

pressing our faces against the icy violet jellyfish
gliding on their eddies and back-draughts
their silken root threads quivering to pulse waves,
pulling against the vortex. Clasping cold fingers

we would eye the hybrid lives of the zoo—
feather-toed hens, dwarf donkeys, kangaroo-rats—
and dream a stampede of roaring ghost animals
in the Tiergarten, on the run from the trains.

The trees in the zoo's park were still frozen
in their early bud, pushing small flowers into air
full of the mewling of unseen birds. Snowflakes
falling on the Spree were tiny gulls.

The yellow U-Bahn took us home, its bulbs rocking,
pale petals fluttering in the arc of its headlamps.

Glyn Maxwell

THE SARAJEVO ZOO

Men had used up their hands, men had
offered, cupped, or kissed them to survive,
had wiped them on the skirts of their own town,
as different men had shinned up a ladder and taken
    the sun down.

One man had upped his arms in a victory U
to a thousand others, to show how much of the past
he did not know and would not know when he died.
Another's joke was the last a hostage heard:
    Oh I lied

which did win some applause from the bare hands
of dozing men. And others of course had never
fired before, then fired, for the work of hands
was wild and sudden in those days
    in those lands.

For men. For the women there was
the stroke, the ripping of hair, the smearing of tears,
snot, and there was the prod of a shaking man,
or with fused palms the gibbering prayer
    to the U.N.

The nothing they had between those palms was
hope and the yard between surrendering palms
was hope as well. Far off, a fist in the sky
was meaning hope but if you prised it open
    you saw why.

The hands of the children here were wringing themselves
hot with the plight of animals over there,
and drawing them in their pens with the crimson rain
of what men do to each other on television
      crayoned in.

But hands continued to feed the demented bear
who ate two other bears to become the last
bear in the Sarajevo Zoo. And they fed him
when they could, two Bosnian zookeepers
      all autumn.

Today I read that that time ended too,
when fifteen rifles occupying some thirty
hands got there and crept in a rank on knees
towards the smoke of the blown and stinking cages
      and black trees.

Trees were what you could not see the starving
beasts behind, or see there were now no beasts,
only the keepers crouching with their two lives.
Then winter howled a command and the sorry branches
      shed their leaves.

Ralph Gustafson

AT THE ZOO

O for all the blind, sadness!
For all men, reminder, reminder,
Light is done, eyes do not see,
Girls walk by grace of others,
Hands reach out, rain falls
And leaves do not show silver, the eyelid
In its workings clears nothing.
Praise, those who count suns.
Children. Children. I think of children
Not used to it, a happening
Of birthdays felt only,
Neither red, nor yellow, nor white
Candles—except the heart convey it.
In this smelly yard, small
Hands discover the elephant, the entire
Enormous building, rumpled skin
Going up forever standing still,
The soft snuff dangerous but the movable
Ears flopped with withdrawals not really.
I watch the stupendous information.
Elephant is said to be there.

COUNTEE CULLEN

THOUGHTS IN A ZOO

They in their cruel traps, and we in ours,
Survey each other's rage, and pass the hours
Commiserating each the other's woe,
To mitigate his own pain's fiery glow.
Man could but little proffer in exchange
Save that his cages have a larger range.
That lion with his lordly, untamed heart
Has in some man his human counterpart,
Some lofty soul in dreams and visions wrapped,
But in the stifling flesh securely trapped.
Gaunt eagle whose raw pinions stain the bars
That prison you, so men cry for the stars!
Some delve down like the mole far underground,
(Their nature is to burrow, not to bound),
Some, like the snake, with changeless slothful eye,
Stir not, but sleep and smoulder where they lie.
Who is most wretched, these caged ones, or we,
Caught in a vastness beyond our sight to see?

Gavin Ewart

THE ANIMALS IN THE ADELAIDE ZOO

The animals in the Adelaide Zoo are very comfortable.
It's a small zoo but very well organized.
The elephant stands in a small space but seems happy.
The black-backed jackals run; hunting, hunting, hunting.
A slow loris moves quiet in nocturnal lighting.
The black panther is a melanistic form of the spotted leopard.

The animals in the Adelaide Zoo are not rhetorical.
The zebras are not torn apart by lions.
The hippopotamus is in happy water.
The giraffe's sex organs are as high as your head.
The jaguars and ocelots attack nothing.
Everything is as it should be in the Adelaide Zoo.

The animals in the Adelaide Zoo are already in Heaven.
Their children are born lucky, nobody hates them.
They are surrounded by love and regular food.
Their lives are without drama, they show no fear.
Eviscerated on a path lies a tiny indigenous mouse.
In their cages, they show no concern, in the Adelaide Zoo.

Gail Mazur

IN HOUSTON

I'd dislocated my life, so I went to the zoo.
It was December but it wasn't December. Pansies
just planted were blooming in well-groomed beds.
Lovers embraced under the sky's Sunday blue.
Children rode around and around on pastel trains.
I read the labels stuck on every cage the way
people at museums do, art being less interesting
than information. Each fenced-in plot had a map,
laminated with a stain to tell where in the world
the animals had been taken from. Rhinos waited
for rain in the rhino-colored dirt, too grief-struck
to move their wrinkles, their horns too weak
to ever be hacked off by poachers for aphrodisiacs.
Five white ducks agitated the chalky waters
of a duck pond with invisible orange feet
while a little girl in pink ruffles
tossed pork rinds at their disconsolate backs.

This wasn't my life! I'd meant to look
with the wise tough eye of exile, I wanted
not to anthropomorphize, not to equate, for instance,
the lemur's displacement with my displacement.
The arched aviary flashed with extravagance,
plumage so exuberant, so implausible, it seemed
cartoonish, and the birdsongs unintelligible,
babble, all their various languages unravelling—
no bird can get its song sung right, separated from
models of its own species.

For weeks I hadn't written a sentence,
for two days I hadn't spoken to an animate thing.
I couldn't relate to a giraffe—
I couldn't look one in the face.

I'd have said, if anyone had asked,
I'd been mugged by the Gulf climate.
In a great barren space, I watched a pair
of elephants swaying together, a rhythm
too familiar to be mistaken, too exclusive.
My eyes sweated to see the bull, his masterful trunk
swinging, enter their barn of concrete blocks,
to watch his obedient wife follow. I missed
the bitter tinny Boston smell of first snow,
the huddling in a cold bus tunnel.

At the House of Nocturnal Mammals,
I stepped into a furtive world of bats,
averted my eyes at the gloomy dioramas,
passed glassed-in booths of lurking rodents—
had I known I'd find what I came for at last?
How did we get here, dear sloth, my soul, my sister?
Clinging to a tree-limb with your three-toed feet,
your eyes closed tight, you calm my idleness,
my immigrant isolation. But a tiny tamarin monkey
who shares your ersatz rainforest runs at you,
teasing, until you move one slow, dripping,
hairy arm, then the other, the other, the other,
pulling your tear-soaked body, its too-few
vertebrae, its inferior allotment of muscles
along the dead branch, going almost nowhere
slowly as is humanly possible, nudged
by the bright orange primate taunting, nipping,
itching at you all the time, like ambition.

Stuart MacKinnon

ON THE WAY TO THE VIVARIUM

We should all wear a baffling agent,
The limpid air cast in folds
In the sun's wake, or by our bodies
Curved to a more definite shape.

Instead we wear the skins of beasts
Enveloped in their stickiness which is
Nearly meaningful, the bull for sex
The yelping dog for his tormentor.

They itch, these skins. That is their graft.
They would become part of us
If we did not strip them like
New scabs from each others' backs.

O the animals we have flayed
To clothe ourselves I poke among,
The rotting carcasses in a shallow pit.
I am looking for one that saved me.

Now that they have nothing but air
To clothe them they are terrible misfits.

Tom Pow

LOVE AT THE (BRONX) ZOO

We walk the icy paths
past frozen ponds, snowed-in enclosures,
where reeds like drifting porcupine
and black huts are all that show.

In the dim warmth of an animal house,
we linger by a tank
with a sandy-coloured,
soft-shelled turtle, the size
of my spread hand. From the long spoon
of its head, nostrils stick out
like tiny binoculars. Eyes,
two silvery stains. When it rises
from the dark green weed, its fins,
like sycamore seeds, brush the window
we peer through. So close is it
and so angled, we see

the thin loop of its down-turned mouth;
almost fancy it would speak…

Back in the Bronx, we don't know
which blind-eyed alley to turn down;
eventually are wrong anyway. We ride around—
a fly caught in deadly nightshade—trying
to reclaim the rim of the highway

past burned-out buildings, waste-ground;
a brazier licking the chill
off some winos.

A battered blue cadillac jerks
to a stop in front of us. Rusted panels
shake; red tail lights glare
from corroded fins. We sit tight
as the black man's black curses plume
into the winter air. We turn to each other—
sudden neophytes, who might—sleepless, speechless,
in the dark cage of night—hold their soft bodies
close; fear
for love's survival.

Carol Ann Duffy

MRS DARWIN

7 April 1852.

Went to the Zoo.
I said to Him—
Something about that Chimpanzee over there reminds me of
   you.

David Ignatow

LOVE IN A ZOO

What I offer she strips
and throws its peelings to the ground,
swallows the bulk in one gulp
and loses me in her stomach,
swinging back and forth by the tail
from a branch. Say to the monkey,
I need you, pat my cheek, kiss my brow.
Tell me it's wonderful to be given
a banana from my hands. Say
that you love me more each day
and do not know how you can survive
without me in the zoo. Say,
Let us make a home together.
Then I will feed you bananas all day
and little monkeys will spring up between us
secure and warm. Monkey, monkey
sends me home, scratching its buttocks
and picking fleas.

Bruce Taylor

ORANGUTANS

We have come here for the peanuts and to meet
the mortified stares of the wild men,
quarantined on their island of packed dirt,
in their crater of painted cement
under the theatrical fork
of a plaster tree.

We have entrusted them with three tires,
a bundle of rope
and as much straw as they can use,

and with a little encouragement
they have manufactured
minute quantities of fun,
twirling a stem of clover,
patting a small pile of dust,
pouring sand over a beetle.

We have also built bleachers for ourselves
to make sure we are comfortable while we wait
for the interesting thoughts
we are planning to have
as we watch what the orangutans
do.

Brian Bartlett

HUTTERITE TWINS TROPICAL

Ropey-limbed gibbons fall through moist air—
rhythms exact as math, hands hooking branches

neatly, just in time. If she grew
such arms, shouts the skinny twin, bouncing

in plain shoes under the glass dome, her voice
frenzied wind-chimes, she'd jump just like that.

"Great Kiskadee Flycatcher!" her sister
chimes in by a sign. "Splendid Glossy Starling!"

Nobody roaming the zoo's mazes raises more noise,
their voices unleashed with the thrill of breaking

laws or finding boys: "Red-Whiskered Bulbul!"
"Hottentot Teal?" "White-Crested Laughing Thrush!"

Their bewildered father worrying his beard,
their motions mimic the spilling brook

near the lords of puddles, the ceremonial-tailed,
the saw-beaked. When birds and birds' ripe names

entice in equal measure, the twins leap—
their eyes wide, wild syllables in their throats.

Al Purdy

IN CABBAGETOWN

On cool nights I would creep
from the Cabbagetown house
on Sackville Street to Riverdale
Zoo with hard-beating heart
entering the monkey cage at 2
a.m. with an orange-bitten moon
over one shoulder and wondering:
"Why should the moon taste good
and to whom?"
          "You you you"
sang the little primates "But
          Quiet Quiet now
the zooman sleeps in his cage of wood
and the wallpaper stars shine thru"
Then they told me about Africa

After the drunks on Parliament Street
released from Winchester pub
like fleas fled fast to their beds
I came
       to the mountain lion's house
in the high dry country of Colorado
at cloud-hung Nimpkish Lake
when the big firs sang the wind
to a silver slurp on Forbidden Plateau
he nuzzled his mother's hairy dugs
that glowed in the dark glowed in the dark
in his head
       He said
          "Tell me why"
the red lights change to green at Queen
& Bay when there's no one about
           —no one about?"
I couldn't say

but the zooman slept nearby
at Toronto Crematorium Brown
and Mackenzie slept their dead
thoughts stopped at 3 a.m.
At 3 a.m.
                the clocks struck Three
                    —Three they said three times

The woman in bed with shoulder bare
and one breast shone like a moon Mare
I left I came
                to the elephant towns
and grey houses on four legs moved
houses the colour of earth rolled by
while Toronto slept and moaned in sleep
the great trunks held me close
And the herd bull said
                        "Tell me of India
tell me of snakes and antelopes
the burning ghats where Ganges shines
I was born here and do not know
Speak about jungle heat
when the tiger's whiskers drip sweat
and the monsoon sighs in Cawnpore night
I can't forget I can't forget
what I have never known"
"Four Four Four Four"
said clocks somewhere

The zooman woke in policeman blue
pointing his sixgun finger at me
"Get Out Get Out" and I
fled back to bed on Sackville Street
in Colorado and Nimpkish Lake
and a wind-sung skein of moon
on the Forbidden Plateau lulled me to sleep
in India and Africa dreaming of
what I can't forget
dreams I have never known—

Carl Sandburg

ELEPHANTS ARE DIFFERENT TO DIFFERENT PEOPLE

Wilson and Pilcer and Snack stood before the zoo elephant.

Wilson said, "What is its name? Is it from Asia or Africa? Who feeds it? Is it a he or a she? How old is it? Do they have twins? How much does it cost to feed? How much does it weigh? If it dies, how much will another one cost? If it dies, what will they use the bones, the fat, and the hide for? What use is it besides to look at?"

Pilcer didn't have any questions; he was murmuring to himself, "It's a house by itself, walls and windows, the ears came from tall corn-fields, by God; the architect of those legs was a workman, by God; he stands like a bridge out across deep water; the face is sad and the eyes are kind; I know elephants are good to babies."

Snack looked up and down and at last said to himself, "He's a tough son-of-a-gun outside and I'll bet he's got a strong heart, I'll bet he's strong as a copper-riveted boiler inside."

They didn't put up any arguments.
They didn't throw anything in each other's faces.
Three men saw the elephant three ways
And let it go at that.
They didn't spoil a sunny Sunday afternoon;
"Sunday comes only once a week," they told each other.

Charles Bukowski

rain or shine

the vultures at the zoo
(all 3 of them)
sit very quietly in their
caged tree
and below
on the ground
are chunks of rotting meat.
the vultures are over-full.
our taxes have fed them
well.

we move on to the next
cage.
a man is in there
sitting on the ground
eating
his own shit.
I recognize him as
our former mailman.
his favorite expression
had been:
"have a beautiful day."

that day, I did.

Matthew Sweeney

THE ZOOKEEPER'S TROUBLES

for Thomas Lynch

Riesfeldt, the zookeeper, was troubled,
so after work, when the rain cleared,
he took himself out to the orchard
and walked there among the apple trees,
in the dreamy silence that precedes dusk,
thinking of the problem that haunted him.
Why hadn't he stayed a rose-gardener?
Roses didn't need regular habits,
but his buck-elephant, Stefan, did
and, despite the soul-food of berries
figs and prunes, by the bushel,
and twenty-two doses of laxative,
Stefan's private complication persisted.
For Riesfeldt's wife it was a sport,
for him it was an incitement to violence,
but he rode this, he was a survivor,
and brought to work the next morning
an abundance of extra-virgin olive oil
which he administered in an enema.
He was not prepared for his success—
the sheer force of Stefan's defecation
knocked him to the ground, his head
hitting a rock, and he lay there
while two hundred pounds of dung
formed a mountain on top of him.
It took hours to clean up the remains.

Linda Pastan

THE KEEPER

In Tintoretto's *Creation
of the Animals*, God
in His beard and robes extends
His great body, arms bent
like the wings of the white swan,
legs doing a kind of scissors-kick,
as if He must try flight
and swimming both, becoming Himself
part of that strange swarm—
each feather and scale and hair made
from the same new paint—
before He can declare them: Good.
It is only the fifth day.
Adam will come later
and generations later still
the keeper I remember at the Bronx Zoo
who sat among the elephants
in his gray and crumpled uniform, trumpeting
with laughter, feeding
them bits of his own lunch,
always taking the first
small taste himself.

A.F. Moritz

ZOO KEEPER

We watched the old zoo keeper,
the tigers sleeping,
haul them in their supper.
We saw him slipping

as he lugged the meat, heavy
and red, in the cage
through urine and water... a gravy
of various sewage

he later mopped up, his joints
snapping: we could hear.
Then he's done and a child points:
the tigers stir,

roused by the closing door's click.
He was gone, forgotten,
as we watched them shamble to lick
their slumped, blood-sodden

food. And I was the keeper
of my own breast.
Did my fierceness go any deeper
than my self-served feast?

Ease, ease, ease
is all I love,
to salve, satisfy, erase
what makes me move.

Miriam Waddington

WONDERFUL COUNTRY

May was a wonderful country;
All the world's children were in pilgrimage
To greet the summer, and on the way
They stopped at the zoo and lifted spells
From the golden tiger and lonely lion,
They appointed zebras their ambassadors
To laughter and they counted rabbits
Surrogates of colour, on the grassy hill
They observed the peacock pondering,
Saw pride was his stature and wrote it off
To beauty which wears a heavy hood
And a light head.
Down in the fen the swans
Glided smooth as music, and the children said:
'Let them be, they will make pillows soft as sleep,
And sleep deep as death.' So the children said,
And let them be.

Around them the city flowed and the children saw
Mandarin yellow leaping at them from coats,
And there were chartreuse and purple—
The lanes were like a bazaar decked out
With romance for the lucky where
Across the hot-dog counter
Beggars and queens came together,
Oh what a clamour and shout under the palace of summer
As the children marched singing hallelujah to May,
Singing homage to May and to meadows.

Woodworm

THE ZOO

And would we like to buy a guide
A souvenir, six ninetynine? Coupons inside?
And can we smell the rain
And the plastic things that smell of rain,
Vicariously, in green-stretched sweat?
Yet, if it dampens like regret, we. can always fumble with the flask
Of vile coffee, and wait in line for the tiny train.

There is a room with wheelchairs, a special room
With tea, and sausage sandwiches, and misted windows
Where small girls look outwards in their wisdom
(Who never felt the need to ask)
Glasses as steamed as the giraffe house
That sunless Sunday of concrete
That Sunblest Sunday of ice-lolly-overkill.

And when the Sunkist sun sicks itself up, a little later,
We can mooch between the tapirs and
The plastic dinosaurs, which are no sillier than
The marmosets in their dripping golden fuzz
Or the shooting-ranch, or the peccaries, or us.

When we were kids, this place seemed a universe, like ours
But slightly skewed, where the slanted sun threw crude
Unruly photographs of shit and straw on us: the strangeness
Of it all: the resigned animals, the unresigned children,
Who saw themselves in all of it:
The cynical optimism, the display,
The naming of the parts: taxonomy, decay,

And ice-creams, and the funfair, with its dome:
The car-park, and that twitching journey home.

Things All Shaped Like Tigers

Margaret Atwood

DREAMS OF THE ANIMALS

Mostly the animals dream
of other animals   each
according to its kind

          (though certain mice and small rodents
          have nightmares of a huge pink
          shape with five claws descending)

: moles dream of darkness and delicate
mole smells

frogs dream of green and golden
frogs
sparkling like wet suns
among the lilies

red and black
striped fish, their eyes open
have red and black striped
dreams   defence, attack, meaningful
patterns

birds dream of territories
enclosed by singing.

Sometimes the animals dream of evil
in the form of soap and metal
but mostly the animals dream
of other animals.

There are exceptions:

the silver fox in the roadside zoo
dreams of digging out
and of baby foxes, their necks bitten

the caged armadillo
near the train
station, which runs
all day in figure eights
its piglet feet pattering,
no longer dreams
but is insane when waking;

the iguana
in the petshop window on St Catherine Street
crested, royal-eyed, ruling
its kingdom of water-dish and sawdust

dreams of sawdust.

Gwendolyn MacEwen

INVOCATIONS

In this zoo there are beasts which
like some truths, are far too true
(clawing ones, and fire-breathers
and flesh-rakers like piranhas
and those that crush the bones to chalk
and those that bare their red teeth in the night)
and some shoot fire to melt the snow
and some chew lazily
on continental shelves,
and some wrap themselves around the world
in an embrace which does not kill
but invents new life around the wound.

Therefore I invoke you, red beast
who moves my blood,
demon of my darker self,
denizen who crawls in my deep want,
white crow, black dove,
eagle and vulture of my love,
and you great buzzard of my dreams,
I call you down
out of yellow rocks and pools of salt,
desert temples hollowed out,
and you white ghost who dwells
in the corner of my eye
to see those things I cannot see
(the broken edges of the air,
the flicker of forms before they occur).

But I invoke you all too well
and you are all too true.
A dragon scares me into heaven,
a fish spits out the continent of Mu,
a big snake recoils and goes to sleep,

I pray the Lord my soul to keep.

Michael Van Walleghen

THE ELEPHANT IN WINTER

During the winter of course
they kept the elephant inside.

His "house," or dungeon really
was practically hidden by brush

and backed up to a small canal
just off the intricate main canal

behind Detroit's Belle Isle Zoo
on which you could skate for miles—

forever, if you happened to forget
in a rattling wind beyond surmise

or earshot of the lost pavilion
just which way you'd come exactly

now that all the trees were dark—
the footbridge wrong completely…

And it's right about here, in little
thudding intervals at first, I felt

the ice begin to move. Okay, sure
I thought: snow trucks. The muffled

banging of some inscrutable pump
or boiler maybe…until, apropos

of nothing but that, a full-grown
male elephant goes suddenly berserk

a scant ten feet away, the whole
five-ton, concussive bulk of him

exploding into high-pitched screams
and a scattering of creeper twigs

every time he throws himself, KA-BOOM!
against the icy wall he lived behind.

That much at least is crystal clear.
But afterwards…I don't know. Perhaps

I fainted or went into shock somehow—
only to be rescued later by wolves…

Or maybe my father showed up finally
blinking his tiny, puzzled headlights

right where he was supposed to meet me
a good two hours ago with the car…

But isn't that the way with children?
Things that must have truly happened

end up blurred, inextricably confused
with dreams—so that, years later

a prized inheritance, a china cabinet
tinkling with the dishes and crystal

my mother only used at Christmas
eerily recalls, as much as anything

that dreamlike moment on the ice…
or the labyrinth, in fact, of home itself—

the angry stirring of the Minotaur
whom I've just woke up somehow

and now, by Christ, he's had enough—
whose least footstep shakes the house.

Peter Meinke

RUNNING WITH THE HYENAS

for Allen Joyce

At 5:00 A.M., in silence, song,
you coast through half-remembered notes,
high, low, white, and black: nightsnow molding
the burrowed city. Though it falls zero
or below, you feel nothing, layered
in old clothes, Vaseline over forehead and nose.
Yours the first steps on the crust, hiss and whisper,
flakes swirl in shallow lamplight, ice thickens
on your whitening beard and the Pleiades
cluster in your chest. You
run, dizzy from childhood, crying with happiness:
First out! First out! But where's your sister,
to make angels in the snow? Now, circling
the park, you wind through the zoo and all sleep,
the lion, white tiger, one-humped dromedary,
where is your father, to name you the names, what
is that shape and whose laughter? Where
is your mother now, so far, so deep?

And suddenly you are not alone: on your left
something is awake, keeping pace in the darkness.
Bodies smudged against snow, across
the moat, they lope grunting beside you so
you turn, and they turn and stay with you,
a grown man, over and over, back and forth
in the zoo; and not for love.

Sasha West

ZOOLOGY

The rhino loves the camel as the camel is the color of the dying grass, the
      muddy stream

and the camel loves the turtle because its shell reflects a dulled sun &
      tarnished moon

and, O, how the turtle loves the bee

but the bee loves only the flower & its own making of honey.

In Houston, all we do is buy: the cast-iron dog who stops the door,

the plastic turtle our children flail about in. The man I love will have

the muzzle of a bear or else he will render his face in plaster, die before us.

The dog loves the moon for being homely & the widow

loves the flowers for having no earthly scent. They swim

like small fishes round the coffin.

The porcupine dreams of sleeping in the elephant's ear, shielded from the
      thunder.

Saint Sebastian loved quills, hunted porcupines until he was one, made by
      arrows.

The painting made him feathered, but not hopeful, and the man I love sank down before it.

He was fond of saying *Time's just that beast whose fur we cling to.*

He was fond of the herds inside my body.

Lisa Olstein

THE HYPNOTIST'S DAUGHTER

At the London Zoo a toddler falls over the rail
of the Primate World *only if you close your eyes*

and a female gorilla comes to sit by, to circle
her long dark arm around him *only this one time*

while the others stay away. The zookeeper says
she lost a baby earlier this year *only just barely*

and they've been waiting months for her tits to dry.
The boy's mother watches from above

only when I say so the thirty minutes it takes
the right person to lower the right ladder down

only as a last resort. In the interim a newscaster
whose station carries it live *only if you promise*

not to let go reports that dolphins and sometimes
certain whales rescue people stranded at sea

only when I close my eyes lift them to the air
when they need breathing or swim them close enough

to land. In the interim I imagine the span of time
from when the smooth hard snout finds me

and begins to push *only if you promise not to tell*
to when we come into view of a shore *only this once*

any shore. In the interim I pray for what should come
to come. I pray for the cat to come out from under

the floorboards *only every once in a while* to come
down from the tall maple, to come back alive

only if you say so in one piece, still in her collar.
I pray to be saved, to be sent far away, to be

allowed to just stay home *only another month or two*
just stay home and erase the objects in each room

with my mind while holding them in my hands
only a matter of time now. I do want to hold them

in my hands, to hold them to my lungs by way
of deep breath *only since July* and a deeper sense

of inhalation. I pray for you o*nly just this once*
to press out from the small veins at the back of my eyes

only you back out into the world. I pray for you
to come and sit by me *only a few more minutes now.*

Sandra Hochman

THE MAMMAL IN CAPTIVITY

I.

He wishes to be remembered
Not as someone who repeated
Observances. Not as a poet,
But as a husband. And when that failed,
A lover. And when that failed,
A tourist with a glass shield in his eyes
Who, for a nickel, took a cruise and saw
The skyline of Manhattan
Carved from blue cinder.
And when that fails,
He prefers to be remembered as a seal,
Simply a mammal who endured his life.
Captivity. Like one of those brown jokers
In the entrance to the zoo: clowning
A little, showing off, sunning, a flap
Of the arms, a lazy snooze, then dive
From rock to pool.
Having no alternative: happily tamed to do
What the mammal in captivity, to save
His skin, must do.

II.

Do not run to the nearest shelter. Awake.
Love is cawing. A particular white crow,
He opens his breast to fly. He dazzles
Us, then preens. Do not run for the nearest shelter.
Awake. For love's a
Black dove all this time. Hairy
And dull, he will hold anything
Between his claws
Preening and devouring our mornings.

III.

This should have been our mornings:
Energetic and believable. Sky
Above our city scratched with beasts,
Ground coffee before speaking. Books
On the tables. Cool water and soap,
And little to be eaten. (Fruit sellers
Scurrying in the streets.) Dressing, working,
Answering the doorbell.
Cleaning. Dusting. Dying.
Then re-birth in the market!
Hoyden things! A hookah pipe, mixture
Of melons, artichokes, sausages, fruit
In every form—rectangles and circles—
Honey with a spine of wax. Fish
In a ribbon catch. Dried onions
And peppers dangling on a line. Centuries
Of cheese spilling milk.

I hear you, like a tame seal,
Barking on a xylophone
Your theme song: *Let me*
Be free one more morning.

Lawrence Ferlinghetti

28

I heard a woman making love today
                              to some beast
Through the wall I heard her voice cry out
                                    in ecstasy
                              or pain or joy
                                 at least
And it was too late
             to do anything about it
                         except go with it
                                    or doubt it
Instead I ran through the streets
                      wearing a mask
                               and singing mad songs
Then fell into a zoo
        tore off my clothes
             and sprang in among the animals
                            those adepts at loneliness
And lay down with them
                      in that unpeaceable kingdom
And fell asleep like a gypsy
                      dreaming of a lioness lover

Jon Anderson

AMERICAN LANDSCAPE WITH CLOUDS & A ZOO

You can be walking along the beach
Of a quaint Northwestern coastal town
On the one hand the great Pacific Ocean
Held placid, restless, in the Sound
When it comes over: like those immense,
Woollen-gray clouds, layer upon layer,
That pour from their Pacific composure
Suddenly troubled, moving, troubling,
Roaring easterly overhead for the inland.
America is in trouble & you're too
Fucked-up to even understand, buy it.
Is America fucked-up because it understands
Itself only too well as you do you?
Every time your girlfriend chucks you
A lusciously coy smile, you're beside
Yourself like a sailboat & every time
You think happiness is just like this,
Forever, you're fooled, like a kid.

America, I'm glad I'm hardly you,
I've got myself to think about.
In my zone is a fairly large zoo,
Plenty of room to walk around; shade,
& the shade that is increasingly, bitterly,
Called shadow. Of animals there are but 2,
Arranged in unpredictable cadence & sequence.
One is the renowned leopard of the snow:
Lazy, humorous, speckled pepper a bit—
Like the wren that flies from shadow to cage
To shade to shadow. When I mistakenly
Awaken at night, I dread both the darkness
& the inevitable increasingly querulous
Birdsong of the inevitable increasingly

Wide stun of light. Everything
Is too brief, eternal, stable, unpredictable.
Everything always says, I'm all there is
Forever, chum, just see it my way, & I do.

Charles O. Hartman

PETTING ZOO

Spring: the edges and middles
of these roads blossom
with corpses, racoon, possum, crow-

lunch, bodies bloomed rosy
into meat and gut, colors
saturated. Eye catching

until the eye learns better.
The slow skunk
lingers in brief afterlife

either because the tail sacs
burst on impact
or because it tried

to warn off what was coming.
Pond turtle crushed to lotus.
Last week the fox flung itself

under my fender—Last week
I hit a fox—Last week my car—
I could make this a poem

about old lovers. I do
worry, slowing down and then
farther down, about being

able to get anywhere.
The thoughtful driver watches
out at all times, maintaining

an easy and natural grip.
I check my fluids weekly,
night after night dream a dim

on-ramp crowded with faint
shapes, fur thick behind
the ears, under my fingers,

my lights, while the back legs jerk
a couple of times. I don't
see for the life of me

how I'd ever end that poem.
My species is all crazy,
think of it, mammals with wheels.

Sylvia Plath

ZOO KEEPER'S WIFE

I can stay awake all night, if need be—
Cold as an eel, without eyelids.
Like a dead lake the dark envelops me,
Blueblack, a spectacular plum fruit.
No airbubbles start from my heart, I am lungless
And ugly, my belly a silk stocking
Where the heads and tails of my sisters decompose.
Look, they are melting like coins in the powerful juices—

The spidery jaws, the spine bones bared for a moment
Like the white lines on a blueprint.
Should I stir, I think this pink and purple plastic
Guts bag would clack like a child's rattle,
Old grievances jostling each other, so many loose teeth.
But what do you know about that
My fat pork, my marrowy sweetheart, face-to-the-wall?
Some things of this world are indigestible.

You wooed me with the wolf-headed fruit bats
Hanging from their scorched hooks in the moist
Fug of the Small Mammal House.
The armadillo dozed in his sandbin
Obscene and bald as a pig, the white mice
Multiplied to infinity like angels on a pinhead
Out of sheer boredom. Tangled in the sweat-wet sheets
I remember the bloodied chicks and the quartered rabbits.

You checked the diet charts and took me to play
With the boa constrictor in the Fellows' Garden.
I pretended I was the Tree of Knowledge.
I entered your bible, I boarded your ark
With the sacred baboon in his wig and wax ears
And the bear-furred, bird-eating spider

Clambering round its glass box like an eight-fingered hand.
I can't get it out of my mind

How our courtship lit the tindery cages—
Your two-horned rhinoceros opened a mouth
Dirty as a bootsole and big as a hospital sink
For my cube of sugar: its bog breath
Gloved my arm to the elbow.
The snails blew kisses like black apples.
Nightly now I flog apes owls bears sheep
Over their iron stile. And still don't sleep.

Lorna Crozier

SANTIAGO ZOO

From her small balcony where she hangs the wash, her son's red jumpsuits, her husband's shirts and socks worn thin at the heels, you can hear the zoo just up the hill. The parrots with their jungle tongues, the scream of monkeys, the old lion's cough. She walks up on Sundays, her little boy's hand clutching his cone so hard it almost breaks. From the top of the hill before smog insinuates its yellow between the streets, she can see the stadium crouching like Yeats' huge beast moving its heavy thighs, already born, its belly barely large enough to hold the dead. In their cages the animals press against the bars, hurting themselves, not to see her and the child, but to gain another inch of sky. Strange what we cage, she thinks, what grace we want worn down, what colours muted, what beauty made smaller than our own. Back in the apartment where the cries of the zoo weave her child's dreams of paradise, it is not the panther escaped from its cell she fears, nor the lion prowling the balcony, picking up the smell of her loved ones, mouthing their clothes. It is the fall of the human foot, the creak of ordinary shoes, the sound the hand makes when it is putting things together or tearing them apart. Tonight on the balcony the noise she hears is only the woman who helps with the housework, humming a song she just heard on the radio, taking the washing in, before the rain.

John Engels

WITH ZIMMER AT THE ZOO

From the very outset
we'd thought we would be late,
from the very first

thought the zoo would soon
be closing, when in truth
it barely had opened, then

through an entire morning
did nothing but stare
at the bull giraffe in his slow

floating run about the moated
enclosure. About noon
a bellowing and caterwaul

arose from the far side of the park
from what must have been
a fierce, considerable beast—

the truth was
the singular animals we were keen to see
were but recently removed

from exhibition, and in
their expensive compounds slept,
and would not be awakened. The truth was,

we would not in the short remainders of our lives
have opportunity to pass this way again
and feared that in our final hours

we'd dream how just at closing
had we possessed courage
and the art, we might

have slipped inside, evaded
the keepers till deep at night
when the zoo awoke to roar its great

and varied chorus to the moon, then stood
close by the shining fence, and loud
in our solitudes, mooed with the Bongo.

Lavinia Greenlaw

HUSH

The Mappin Terraces, 1913

The timber frame of a helter-skelter
smoothed over like the scandal
of the imperial wireless contract
the ministers insisted Marconi won.

A concrete cover-up
to make a mole hill of a mountain.
Gandhi arrested. The King's horse
lost on Emily Davidson.

Each bear prowled its slice of hill
as if it were inside a wheel; to stay still
would be to backslide or sidestep.
Everyone was doing the foxtrot.

Dancers, anglers, children's friends,
fractious, wary, teeth and claws
extracted. The Lords tried twice
to stop the Irish Home Rule Bill.

The last horsedrawn omnibus in Paris
failed to make it through the winter.
There were no bears in the Armory Show,
no bears in *Sons and Lovers* or *Le Grand Meaulnes*.

Robert Kroetsch

THE WINNIPEG ZOO

yes, I am here, exhausted, a wreck, unable
to imagine the act of writing, unable to imagine

I am here, it is quiet, I am exhausted from
moving, we must take care of our stories

the moving is a story, we must take care, I am
here, I shall arrive, I am arriving, I too

have waited, the way in is merely the way,
she takes her lovers, reader, listen, be careful

she takes her lovers one by one to the Winnipeg
zoo, she winds her hair on her fingers, the hook

in the ceiling holds the plant, the ivy climbs
to the floor, must is the end

of winter, the ride to the zoo, the sun on the
man at the gate, the hair wound on her fingers

she takes her lovers, first, the startled boy
stares at the pink flamingos, they rest, folding

one leg at a time, the standing boy, she returns
alone from the Winnipeg zoo, her brown eyes

misting into calm, the hook in the ceiling
holds the plant, what matters is all that matters

the man at the gate says nothing, the kiss of
the Canada lynx, the lightning touch of the snake

is hot, love is round, thumbs are still fingers,
we must take care of our stories, the reptiles

waiting, do not move, flamingos have no names,
the boy, the tall young man, reaching to find her

hand, the polar bear dives deep, into the coiling
water, Audubon raises his gun, the artist

the owl is master of sleep, don't follow,
she takes her lovers past the pond

the farmer from Delacroix, the one who grows
asparagus spears, the one who feeds gourmands

is watching the reptiles, he does not move,
we must take care of our stories, or what it is

is only this, thumbs are still fingers, always,
after an early lunch, the zoological garden

the secret is in the ketchup bottle, the farmer
has short toes, red hair, he wears blue shoes

the man at the gate is not counting, a trickle of
gold at her neck, no wind, her scattered love

is round, Audubon raises his gun, the cranes
reply to the wild turkeys, always, after

an early lunch, the farmer, his hands to the glass,
it is quiet, reader, listen, she comes back alone

flamingos have no names, monkeys learn by hanging,
the lawyer, cracking sunflower seeds, spits

at the watching tiger, he reaches to take
her hand, the popcorn vendor winks

at a scalding baby, somewhere, rococo,
a killdeer furrows the air, the lawyer

cracking sunflower seeds, spits at the tiger's
yellow eyes, but cannot quite imagine

the artist, Audubon, dipping the beaded sight
into the flattened v on the gun's barrel, we must

take care, the sun is a fish,
monkeys learn by hanging, the lizard is only

half asleep, write on the post card, quickly,
I am here, yes, I want to go home, the man

at the gate is not counting, Audubon dips the
beaded sight into the flattened v on the gun's

barrel, the lawyer, cracking sunflower seeds,
the tiger blinks, politely, I am here

exhausted, she is with me, the artist,
Audubon, tightens his index finger

her eyes mist into a calm, the elk
in the distant pasture raises his rack

then it is done, the ducks in the duck pond
cannot fly, the sun sticks out its shadow

we must take care of our stories, I am ex-
hausted from moving, it is quiet, I am here

Diane Wakoski

THE BIRDS OF PARADISE BEING VERY PLAIN BIRDS

"What do they look like," he said.
I said, "They are very very plain,
until they ruffle their neck feathers."

This is a city where
beauty is
unexpected.

They threw the jaguar a dead rabbit,
whole, white, long ears still warm,
pink eye holes in his soft rabbit head;
feeding time at 3 p.m.,
the animals all waiting for their fresh meat;
the jaguar holding the rabbit in his thick paws,
started with the head, working a hole open until
he had the brains exposed, and he continued to lick,
eating at the red mass, until I heard the woman next to me
saying, "I suppose it's natural, but it's so horrible,"
and another saying, "Look how he's got the brains all at once,"
and I, having sat there a whole hour on the bench in the lion house
watching the families walking about
looking at all the great cats, the black leopard,
the lion with her two cubs, the two large jaguars,
felt myself dead and limp, felt myself the rabbit,
thrown into the cage, foolishly, Romantically,
having just before visited the monkey house and watched the
beautiful, dark, white-crested Diana monkies with their grey beards
neurotically run in circles about the cage, touching,
as in a ritual, a certain spot on the wall each time around,
and thinking how cage life drove an animal into mazes of himself,
his cage mates chosen for him, his life circumscribed and focused
on eating, his play watched by it-doesn't-matter-whom, just
watched, always watched. I felt myself there too,

maudlin and sentimental, I felt myself in each place—
the lonesome panda, Chi-Chi,
picking at her foot, soft dirty fur,
alone, sitting aimlessly picking at her foot,
the sea-lion from 40 degrees of latitude trying to get some sun here at
50 degrees of latitude
the buddha mountain goat staring out from the
rocks,
the mountains
that weren't even above sea-level;

curiously,
you felt the desperation of the jaguar
in the cage
who had nothing to divert him,
no steaming jungle path,
no trees to crouch in,
no brush to stalk through,
no deer at the water hole to watch,
no bell bird to ring through the night, as he changed the colors of
his eyes,
who had not even a live rabbit to chase, nor anywhere to chase it,
but dead, fresh-dead, rabbit, thrown to him, limp,
easy to lick the steaming brains from...

A different sun shines on this place,
colder perhaps from a different direction,
like a lemon in a glass pretending it gives light,
a sun that dashes all hope of relationship with the hot sun,
continues his chilly breath,
a sun I might find unrolling itself as a ball of wool,
when I look up into the sky for it.
A sun that might stand behind the pillar of the house next door,
rather than say hello to me as I pass by,
a shy neighbor, you might say,
but really a different sun,
not the one composed of flaming gases I read about in
astronomy books.

"Look at that hearse with the yellow flowers on it," she said,
but her friends on the bus did not see what she saw,
and she looked again, to find a beige colored truck with sacks of
potatoes on its roof. It happens all the time, I told her,
some of us have bad vision, are crippled, have defects, and
our reality is a different one, not the
correct and ascertainable one,
and sometimes it makes us dotty and lonely
but also it makes us poets.
Some people take drugs to change their ascertainable vision
into this cracking one, and we look at the honeycomb floor
and wonder why the head always aches, the belly always
holds a bit of nausea.
We know where the reality is, don't we?

That always causes a long pause.

"Look at that truck with all those sacks of potatoes," she said,
but her friends in the limousine did not know what she was saying,
she was out of her senses, perhaps with grief,
the hearse with the yellow flowers on it travelling too slowly in
the sunlight, the day too slow, too still, the day
when everyone's vision cracked a bit with the sun,
the strain of the bird flying through the window,
the Bird of Paradise suddenly ruffling his feathers,
a change to beauty.

The buddha-goat, big-horned mountain sheep,
sitting staring—one could imagine his eyes as blue
as yours. What does a mountain goat with false mountains
in a city zoo think,
sitting all day, not moving. What do you
think, staring at this expensive ugly wallpaper,
sitting still, in this city, not talking,
the Buddha-Shepherd,
a sheep in his fake mountains.
Eyes so blue.

A dream: lungs.
Lying on the plate with thick crockery the delicate lungs
heaving with unvacated breath,
the jaguar walking around the table
and the Buddha-sheep sitting above, outside
the window, outside the mountain,
staring at the lungs, struggling fish...

A patient dying of cancer will have
lost the sensation of pain in many parts of the body.
Smoking a cigarette
he may not notice it burning through his fingers.
Sitting on a blade, he might not feel it slice his body in half.
Tenderness for the oblivion the Buddha needs,
someone to understand that he has faced all of space and eternity;
it riddles him with pockets and cell-groups of infinity, and does he
feel what is happening now? He stares past himself,
ignoring me.
He says the ear is no good here, neither
is the eye. False mountains
the habitat a dream.

No Birds of Paradise, he also tells me
in other zoos he's seen. What do they look like?
Each has a different look, I say,
but all plain,
very plain, until that ruffling starts.

Once again he is the Buddha sheep,
staring past me into the mirror, his wisdom, mazes of himself,
I the rabbit, never having run in the fields or stolen carrots from
Farmer Brown, raised in a cage,
bred for food,
crouching especially timid but not moving,
the day the keepers came in to wring necks, the hunt never starting,
having been already over at the start
    —the brains go first,
      a hungry animal licking his way down,

    through the red mass,
    no longer a brain.

The Birds of Paradise have only an occasional
and unpredictable
beauty.

Elizabeth Bishop

SLEEPING ON THE CEILING

It is so peaceful on the ceiling!
It is the Place de la Concorde.
The little crystal chandelier
is off, the fountain is in the dark.
Not a soul is in the park.

Below, where the wallpaper is peeling,
the Jardin des Plantes has locked its gates.
Those photographs are animals.
The mighty flowers and foliage rustle;
under the leaves the insects tunnel.

We must go under the wallpaper
to meet the insect-gladiator,
to battle with a net and trident,
and leave the fountain and the square.
But oh, that we could sleep up there....

Wallace Stevens

ANALYSIS OF A THEME

THEME

How happy I was the day I told the young Blandina of three-
legged giraffes . . .

ANALYSIS

> In the conscious world, the great clouds
> Potter in the summer sky.
> It is a province—
>
> Of ugly, subconscious time, in which
> There is no beautiful eye
> And no true tree,
>
> There being no subconscious place,
> Only Indyterranean
> Resemblances
>
> Of place: time's haggard mongrels.
> Yet in time's middle deep,
> In its abstract motion,
>
> Its immaterial monsters move,
> Without physical pedantry
> Or any name.
>
> Invisible, they move and are,
> Not speaking worms, nor birds
> Of mutable plume,
>
> Pure coruscations, that lie beyond
> The imagination, intact
> And unattained,

Even in Paris, in the Gardens
Of Acclimatization,
On a holiday.

The knowledge of bright-ethered things
Bears us toward time, on its
Perfective wings.

We enjoy the ithy oonts and long-haired
Plomets, as the Herr Gott
Enjoys his comets.

Daryl Hine

THE MARCHÉ AUX PUCES AND
THE JARDIN DES PLANTES

The sight of beauty simply makes us sick:
There are too many hours in the day,
Too many wicked faces built like flowers
And far too many bargains for a song.
Jade and paste, cashmere and ormolu—
Who said that all the arts aspire to music?
It's obvious, for time is obvious,
That all that art aspires to is junk.

Blackmailed by these mathoms of the past,
One is indebted for another perspective
To quaint giraffes and quainter wallabies,
The nearly human and the faintly monstrous,
The outrageously contemporary joke.
Trespassing on a no man's territory,
Unlike the moralist one is at a loss
Where to be human is not to be at home.

In a zoo, you see, one can acquire nothing:
Zebras aren't wishes. Nor is the flea market
Exactly the place for those who know what they want.
Like far out stations on the Metro (which they are)
Somewhere, in heaven perhaps, they correspond,
In the heaven of open arms and unpaid bills,
Where beer is drunk on the lawn all afternoon
And every night we bid, and make, a slam.

W.S. Di Piero

LEAVING BARTRAM'S GARDEN IN SOUTHWEST PHILADELPHIA

Outside the gate, the scrawny trees look fine.
New-style trolleys squeak down Woodland
past wasted tycoon mansions and body shops.

There's something I wanted to find,
but what? Roses two months from now
on these brambles? The same refinery fires

lashing over the Schuykill? The adult hand
that held mine here so many years ago?
None of this happened. Across Spring Garden Bridge,

zoo elephants clicked past my window—
birds jumped from dust igniting on their backs.
Inside Bartram's house, elephant-eared

cure-all comfrey leaves hung above the hearth.
A redbird gashed the sunned mullioned glass.
I'm in the weave. The brown-brick project softens

in the sun. Stakes in its communal garden catch
seed packets and chip bags blown across the rows.
Tagger signatures surf red and black

across the wall, fearless, dense lines
that conch and muscle so intimately
I can't tell one name from another.

Roberta Hill

IN THE MADISON ZOO

No rooster wakes them. A donkey brays
in blue dawn air. She never sleeps.
Lake Wingra snares the lilies,
hurries the morning star. The white down
of her talons sheds the city heat.
Far more terrible than lions, smooth pain stone
I cannot leave. A Kodiak in peanuts, paper,
thinks of seals from a long past hunger.
Sky like first day ice. White wings
for bitter ambush, stiff and rimmed with iron.
When she hoots, hide hands in pockets. Such luck
will tear down cobwebs near the stars. What thin bone
rings when I see you, Owl? Waterbugs dream
in knots and whirlpools. I hear music
from railroad evenings.
Town lights blink through the leaves.

Somewhere a fire brightens on the plain.
In the big oak behind the house, amber eyes
crowd my rooms. She hums, while her dress
wraps its tattered edge around the trunk. Arrogant, wise,
she calls me out from this dusty window where voices
try to hold the cup and saucer still.
Sparrow-bound to rain, I remember a cage
under younger trees.

There the cottonwoods rattle and thirst.
She's the only light in tunnelled black.
If I were to leave, my house would burn.
They would find me thrashing in the weeds
with a face of sand. Changed by a glance,
I haunt the fierce wet hills, press the granite roots
to reach a sound, rich as thunder,
bright and fleeting as the path of a snail.

Randall Jarrell

THE WOMAN AT THE WASHINGTON ZOO

The saris go by me from the embassies.

Cloth from the moon. Cloth from another planet.
They look back at the leopard like the leopard.

And I. . . .
        this print of mine, that has kept its color
Alive through so many cleanings; this dull null
Navy I wear to work, and wear from work, and so
To my bed, so to my grave, with no
Complaints, no comment: neither from my chief,
The Deputy Chief Assistant, nor his chief—
Only I complain. . . . this serviceable
Body that no sunlight dyes, no hand suffuses
But, dome-shadowed, withering among columns,
Wavy beneath fountains—small, far-off, shining
In the eyes of animals, these beings trapped
As I am trapped but not, themselves, the trap,
Aging, but without knowledge of their age,
Kept safe here, knowing not of death, for death—
Oh, bars of my own body, open, open!

The world goes by my cage and never sees me.
And there come not to me, as come to these,
The wild beasts, sparrows pecking the llamas' grain,
Pigeons settling on the bears' bread, buzzards
Tearing the meat the flies have clouded. . . .
        Vulture,
When you come for the white rat that the foxes left,
Take off the red helmet of your head, the black
Wings that have shadowed me, and step to me as man:
The wild brother at whose feet the white wolves fawn,
To whose hand of power the great lioness
Stalks, purring. . . .
        You know what I was,
You see what I am: change me, change me!

Mary di Michele

INVITATION TO THE DNA ZOO

The body is a crowded zoo. In the *Jardin des Plantes*,
Paris, 1907, as if from behind bars, the poet
paces along with the panther, following its inward
spiral until, arriving at the centre of the cage, he

disappears. Angels in the aviary.
Under the skin there is fur.
Under the skin there is another
skin, a coat, lined in red
mink. Listen.

What is it? Simian or snake or something in
between, mewling in the spine?

Alvin Greenberg

34

we are that stuffed cat that guards the hats
in the london haberdasher's window where
you stood five rainy minutes trying to decipher
us. well, we're alive, always alive because that's
what you need us to be, windowsful of exhibits
at the natural history museum, bison, saber-
toothed tiger ready to spring, even poor trigger
in roy roger's living room. you think it's
easy, you who were there at the cincinnati zoo
when the earth's last passenger pigeon bought it?
duty, that's what: your own dead you can fling
into the earth, but we always have to be with you:
that small pile of bones in the back of the closet
or out of the melting glacier, the unnameable *thing*.

Eavan Boland

PRISONERS

I saw him first lost in the lion cages
Of the zoo; before he could tear it out
I screamed my heart out; but his rages
Had been left behind. All he had left was his lope,
His mane, as bored as a socialite
With her morning post, I saw him slit
A rabbit open like an envelope.

Everything after that was parody—
I glimpsed him at the hearth in a jet
Cat, in a school annual tamed in type,
In a screen safari. The irony
Of finding him here in the one habitat
I never expected, alive and well in our suburban
World, present as I garden, sweep,

Wring the teacloth dry, domesticate
Acanthus in a bowl, orbit each chair
Exactly round our table. Your pullover
Lies on the bed upstairs, spread there where
You can no more free yourself from the bars
Of your arms round me than can over
Us the lion flee, silently, his stars.

Lisa Jarnot

THEY LOVED THESE THINGS TOO

The sun the moon the stars the polar ice caps and the ice cream cones the city streets the side streets and the small TV the curve of flesh around the food the road maps and November and the tiny birds and also certain people and they loved the special chairs and also stuffed things and the carnival and big rings and the o rings and they loved the oranges in bags and Florida and Texas and the hotel room and they loved the chili on the highway that they loved as if they loved the onramp and the way that people called and the natural forces of destruction and the sea they loved the sea and also boats and sailing ships and whales they loved and sea birds in varieties and then they loved the choice of drinks to drink and also beer they loved the times that others liked them that they loved and also they loved things all shaped like tigers and they loved the zoo.

Permissions

~

Acknowledgements

Special thanks to two research assistants whose work proved invaluable: Sachiko Murakami laid eyes upon many of these poems before we did, and read a great deal of zoo fiction in the early stages of research; Susan Paddon saw the anthology through its final pre-publication year, a year of myriad permissions requests, proofreading tasks, and final decisions, all of which she handled admirably.

Thank you to all those who put us in touch with zoo poets, and to those who suggested poems that might be of interest. Brian Bartlett particularly deserves a mention for recommending a slew of excellent zoo poems, and Nancy Holmes' shared discoveries saved us many hours of research.

Dominic Davies kindly granted us permission to use his "Hippo, Rotterdam" on our cover free of fees, for which we are very grateful.

Finally, and most essentially, thanks are due to the Social Sciences and Humanities Research Council of Canada and the Fonds québécois de la recherché sur la société et la culture, without whose generous support this anthology would not exist.

Author Index

Signal
EDITIONS

Carmine Starnino, Editor
Michael Harris, Founding Editor

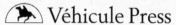 Véhicule Press